The Pleasure Principle

THE PLEASURE PRINCIPLE

Jon Loomis

Oberlin College Press

www.oberlin.edu/~ocpress

Publication of this book was supported in part by a grant from the Ohio Arts Council.

Ohio Arts Council
A STATE AGENCY
THAT SUPPORTS PUBLIC
PROGRAMS IN THE ARTS

Cover image: René Magritte, "Le Principe du Plaisir," 1937.
© 2001 C. Herscovici, Brussels/Artists Rights Society (ARS), New York.

Library of Congress Cataloging-in-Publication Data

Loomis, Jon
        The Pleasure Principle / Jon Loomis.
        (The FIELD Poetry Series v. 11)
        I. Title.   II. Series.

LCCN: 2001095677
ISBN: 0-932440-90-8   (pbk.)

for Chet

CONTENTS

ONE

TWO

THREE

ONE

Romance: A Parable

I live in a garden apartment. Upstairs, a woman I rarely see,
who keeps a huge leggy dog and a green parrot. Every day
an hour after she walks to work, the parrot calls from its cage

at the kitchen window—*Dinnertime!*—in the woman's throaty alto.
Every day the dog leaps up from its rug in the bedroom, gallops
down the hall—clawing and skidding around the turn

at the kitchen door, a lion-colored haunch bashing into the wall—
the whole house quivering. You can almost hear the dog's
confusion; almost see it snuffle the empty bowl,

sit and ponder beneath its furrowed brows before tick-ticking
back to the rug, where it sighs and falls asleep. Pleased with itself
the parrot cackles and shrieks a while and then falls silent.

I imagine it cocking a bright, malicious eye. Outside, traffic
rumbles down the brick street. The mailman whistles on the stoop,
stuffs a wad of catalogs through the slot. Then the parrot calls again—

Dinnertime! Dinnertime!— the dog erupts down the hall, caroms
off the door, snuffles, click-clicks slowly back to its rug and lies down.
Some days the parrot tricks the dog again and again. Each time

the dog forgets. Optimist, what else can she do? Pretend to sleep?
Pretend that something lovely isn't waiting in the other room?

The Pleasure Principle

We are failed agnostics, so many moments
of conviction. Even this midwestern
sunrise moves us—Rothko strip of pink

above the Poultry Lab. All appetite,
all sweat and dander, what keeps us
from the neighbors' throats

(their garden gnomes, their damned
dog barking)? Maybe just this labial glow,
the way the lake ice mutters and booms…

It's early, cold out. These bodies
are nothing, wear them once
and throw them away—

but they're *good* nothing. Your warm neck,
small snore. Roomful of salmon light.
Night unzipping its sequined gown.

Sin

Rosh Hashanah, sun licked and stuck
to the sky's blue envelope. Late September slant
of light across the lake. We're feeding the ducks—

stale baguette, the old year's terrible crumbs.
Think of your sins, you say. Where to start? Envy,
of course. Sloth—the muse upstairs, mouthing her gun.

And, since I was five, caught in the dress-shop
looking up the mannequin's skirts—this love
for the bodies of women (armpit, downed nape,

crease between pubis and thigh). Innocent
of everything, the ducks know only their hunger,
gabbling after every morsel, green necks outstretched.

Feel better? you ask. The wind picks up. Leaves float
bright in the lake's blue universe. *Like a new man*
I say, and it's almost true—for a moment I'm flayed,

salted clean. Walking back, the curve of your ankle,
the small sway of your hips. Lucky we're out of bread.
The lake would boil. The trees would run from its banks.

You Blow Out the Candles

and here comes middle age, with its bad breath
and heartburn, swollen prostate, platinum card.
Middle-age, pouchy and liminal. What you get

if you're lucky—twenty years of halfway.
All the men on my father's side drop dead
at sixty-five, martini glasses clutched,

heels drumming someone's persian rug. Halfway
and then some. Thirty-nine, what have I done
with my life? The usual longings, song after song

of my suburban self. If I could start over
I'd live in Memphis, learn to play the pedal steel—
enough free verse, enough New England ghost moon,

ghost woods—all night the smallpox quarantines,
mouths full of leaf rot, scuffing down the bike path
in their buckled shoes. There's too much history

out here, mine and everyone else's, too many poets
cranking it out—*magenta sunset, beech forest
canopy on fire, the bay and Pilgrim Lake*

on fire, on fire... Enough, already.
Here we go, any minute now—me and my body
off to the gym. Not quite the company I wished for—

me and old bald spot. Soft gut. Sore knee.

Longing

All day you've thought of nothing
but her nipped waist, the sweet
tilt of her hips. Evening,

grading papers, you still can't concentrate—
your wife reads in the next room;
outside, tulips clench in the half-light,

the lawn sizzles, delirious with rain.
It's grim, turning forty: ear hair, arrhythmia—
God's little bag of gag gifts. And now

infatuation, coming just as it did
at seventeen, skunked dog
at the cocktail party, pink tongue

dangling. If only it wasn't Spring.
If only the rain would stop,
and starlings weren't distracting

the poplar tree, and the daffodils would shut
their yellow mouths. Maybe you could
get some work done, join your wife

in her cool bed. Maybe you could sleep
and never dream of anything again.

Epithalamial

There is the rain which stops, then the steaming
absence of its long applause. There are crows
on the rooftops, chuckling low in their throats—

their secret language. I wanted to tell you
good luck, all the best; the usual lies. I wanted
to tell you what Tu Fu said—something wise

and oblique about wind, and the light
on a green hill. Wet grapevine fingers
the deck chairs, tongues the black enamel

of the Weber grill. All summer long, the city smells
like piss. Not what you want to hear, I know—
back in Ohio, moist in your silk dress.

Addictions

Dawn flutters its bruised eyelid.
Torqued sideways, bellies pink-struck,

gulls hang-glide above the Yankee Mart
yelping like manic dogs. Last night

in the dream, we kissed—my wife walking in
just as I slipped my hand inside your blouse.

We sleep, obsessions unspooling,
the mind's little video nattering on—

I still dream of lighting a cigarette,
fifteen years since I quit.

We sleep, if we're lucky.
Then we wake up. The Pilgrim Tower

vamps in its gown of fog. All this time,
you're still making trouble—blue drift

in the lamplight; dark seed in the lungs.

Conversion

After the rain, a sudden bloom
of flies; slow at the window,
they want the silk green

light outside—the *punk, punk*
of hard, furred bellies against the glass
raising your armhair,

what's left of it, what the nurse
didn't shave before she stuck
the needle deep in the dark well

of your blood. Conversion
they call it, the moment your heart
skips back to its old pentameter,

neoformal limp
across the monitor's black screen—
no more syncopation, squirm

in your chest, tight little nut
in the back of your head.
Strapped down, electrodes

peeled and stuck,
i.v. in your right forearm,
oxygen tube in your nose—

you want to feel the shock—
mule kick in the chest,
your body's clench

and flop. But no—you're drugged,
zapped, sent home, no memory
of anything, no souvenir

but the gauze taped to your arm,
two itching burns
on your chest and back—

and somehow, scribbled
on a Pfizer post-it,
a number you'll never call

(the nurse, whose face
you can't remember),
which you'll find, years from now,

tucked into your copy
of *China Trace*—alone
in the quiet house, glass of scotch,

rain on the skylight…
Fool, you could have led
an altogether different life.

Happiness

Night. Crickets
winding their watches.
Summer burning out

at last, the lawn scorched,
the big catalpa slowly
stripping down to scabs.

A spider rappels
from the ceiling fan.
A chartreuse tree-frog's

glued to the screen,
haloed in moths.
The house settles

an eighth of an inch—
deep in their burrows
the fire ants rejoice.

Balthus Returns

Clever, as marmots go. Piercing whistle,
delicate paws. Outside, the garden's

tunnelled, the lawn's hummocked and drilled.
When he tires of digging, he paints. All day,

all night the models clomp up and down the stairs
in their maryjanes—young girls, eyes glazed,

slack-jawed and stumbling. He paints them nude
or partly nude, legs fanned wide, heads lolling.

One day, soldiers round up all the giant rodents.
Safe in Switzerland, the marmot isn't gassed—

he burrows, paints his drugged adolescents
as if nothing has changed—his lost cat Mitsou

leering from every canvas, sprawled on a table,
perched on a ladderback chair. *Darling Boy*,

writes Rilke—the great poet, brought up
in ringlets, crisp little dresses. *Darling Boy*

how I've missed you. The marmot rolls his eyes,
balls the letter into the fire. Smooths his whiskers.

Turns to the slender twelve-year-old, supine
on the sofa. You are so lovely in this light

he says. Please, *alouette*, lift your skirt
just a little. Let me help you unbutton your blouse...

Russian Novel

Snowfall, the fields button
their white trousers. Sasha smokes
on the terrace. Inside, the fire leaps,

the orchestra tweedles a waltz.
The beauty! I'm in love with beauty—
silk gown, dropped glove—

I'm giddy with dancing, champagne,
I'm weak with candlelight, in love
with falling in love with love…

Snowfall. The village steams.
Peasants grunt in their huts.
Stiff in his uniform (crisp white

trousers), Sasha smokes his black
cheroot—handsome, moustaches
soft as silk. Betrothed at twelve,

soon we're to wed—such waltzing!
Champagne! Such grunting
of peasants in huts! Snowfall,

artillery crunch in the distance.
Sasha smokes on the terrace,
pale in his bandage, trickle of blood

from his boot. Soon we're to wed,
giddy with dancing. The peasants
will rattle their collars,

the orchestra tweedle and groan—
such waltzing! Such beauty! Such love!

Millennial

Not a good start, not a good sign
when the Pier One parking lot
yawns, sucks your BMW

down its dark throat (car alarm
hooting, cell phone's dwindling
chirp). August, Atlanta shimmers

and fades in the dogwood-tops.
The sky rips its green trousers—
a torrent of eels tumbles out.

So much to atone for—the rapture
come and gone with its shop-vac.
We're still here, still sawing away

at this roast haunch of neighbor.
Later, we'll frolic like seals
in his pool, dance naked all night

on his dark, impeccable lawn…

Skinnydipping, Late Summer

Rachel laughs, hovering nude
in the pool's blue blur.
It's late, two a.m.,

you've been drinking scotch
but still your teeth chatter,
the water a cold robe

you slip into, testicles
burrowing deep in their fur.
You shouldn't be here—

not quite unfaithful, your wife
a thousand miles away.
Moonrise in the east,

tangerine slice.
Mosquitos sipping your blood
through delicate straws.

Rachel floats on her back,
nipples aimed at the sky—
the stars' bright clutter and smear.

She's so young.
The water's a kind of amnesia
(forget your middle-aged belly,

your wife, your heart
which flutters and dives).
Soon, the world will click

to a slow stop—everything
spinning away. The last falling
stars in the treetops. One last

slim girl, slick fish
swimming into your arms.

After the Rapture

Quiet, now that you're gone.
Out at Race Point, the waves mince
and subside. If I were a dead seal

the gulls would tug my eyes
from their crimson shells,
the green crabs would polish my ribs.

Less useful, I wait in a slatted chair.
Day-moon, thin slice of onion—
grackles convene in the courtyard,

hungry as poets, prismatic.
Three days since I've spoken, except
to the neighbor's cat (so much time,

cat, so little worth saying)—
childless, divorced, what do I know
about anything? Not where this line

of red ants is going; not even
the name of the pink-flowered tree.
What would I say if the Judgment came,

God licking his fingertip, turning
my page? *What was the question?*
Sorry… Mostly I slept…

On the First Tee with Charles Wright

My tee shot is a paltry thing, a low slow dribbler—80 yards
but almost straight, and almost in the fairway. Charles nods

and shrugs—he's seen worse, and being from the South
is too polite to say what David says: "Hey, Loomis—

have your husband hit it for you." Charles takes a practice swing;
smooth and easy, no big deal. "What are those?" he asks, frowning

down the hill. "Catalpas?" We don't know, hadn't noticed them,
had not until this moment smelled the pine-sap or the leaf-rot,

hadn't thought too much about the light, and how this time
of year it rises from the tall red grass beside the highway

like redemption—hell, we haven't even read *Cathay*. Charles hits
his drive a mile but veering left, toward a pond, and then—I swear

this much is true—it turns in mid-air, bounces off an alder tree,
rolls an easy pitch from the green. "Look at that," he says.

"I must be living right." And as we walk to our second shots
the clouds above him part, a shaft of violet light descends

and draws him up, still toting his clubs in their canvas bag,
still considering the trees, and he's gone—the sky closed gasket tight

and rippling, a sudden wedge of starlings overhead. "I'm not
surprised," says David, bumping up his lie in the short rough.

"Not after a shot like that." But even I can see that golf
is just the metaphor—it could be anything. A parking place.

Steamed crabs and beer. My ex-wife, combing her long black hair.

Uncle Chester's Second Wife

I'm eighteen, traveling east, my first summer
away from home. I've stopped for a few days

in Baltimore, my uncle's house—cat smell
of the boxwood hedge, cicadas tuning their engines

all afternoon in the hemlock tree. No one approves
of Cathy, the new wife. She's thirty, smokes

Virginia Slims, gives me a sweating gin
and tonic, a bosomy hug hello. They're nothing

like my parents. They listen to Hendrix.
Chet wears a pendant, slicks back his hair.

After we eat, he rolls a fat joint. *Jamaican*,
he says, and we smoke it. I go to bed stoned.

2
Stack of Playboys in the guest room, *Justine*,
The Story of O. It's hot—I'm eighteen,

what else would I do? Find the Girls
of the Big Ten, kick back the sheet.

I'm almost done when Cathy walks in.
She squeaks, I cover myself with a pillow,

she drops her armload of towels, scuttles out,
slams the door. And stands awhile in the hallway.

Taps a cigarette out of the pack. It's humid—
at first the match won't light, but then it spits

and flares. Cathy exhales. The glass doorknob
turns. *Listen*, she says, stepping back in,

one side of her lipstick too wide for her mouth.
You don't have to stop. I mean, it's fine with me.

She leans against the closed door, one hand
on the dresser, blue smoke uncoiling.

I'm still stiff as a tusk. She doesn't budge,
doesn't touch me. I do it myself, cicadas revving

and stalling—not even the ghost of a breeze.
When I'm through, she hands me a towel.

Kisses me once, her tongue in my mouth.
And then she says *Sorry, God, I'm so sorry.*

Next morning, early, I hurl myself into my Plymouth,
rumble away—Chet and Cathy afloat on their waterbed,

hangovers brewing. Years later, here's the part
I go back to, the part I still don't get: how to live

in these bodies—follicles, skin mites, fungus and gas.
Literal creatures. What sweet destruction they hold.

Two

Tourists

The Pilgrims landed here in 1620, camped
five weeks, then sailed off to Plymouth—
the first tourists. Month of rain,

no wonder they left—dune grass draggled,
the sea pitched and pale. Month of rain.
Each day I zip my body on again,

feed the neighborhood cat
outside, under the eaves (everything drips—
picnic table, cedar trees, someone's yellow shirt

abandoned on the line). *There is no country
more profoundly dreary*, Thoreau said
after his long walk—tip of the continent's

curly tail, nothing to eat but salt-cod and beans.
Narrow country. Country of rain.
Out in the garden, the dead sunflowers

shudder and lean—black bones of August,
a nuthatch picks at their drooped heads.
Like them, when we're dead

we're not really dead—or so the Book
of Terrible Promises promises. In two months
the seals come back to Herring Cove, haul out

on the beach—a dozen thick-furred yams.
The sand eels come back, the coots,
the humpback whales—fluke silhouettes

in the green distance. But not us—
we're off to the afterlife in our white suits,
sipping our cocktails of light. *Remember*

that country? we'll say. *Country of rain,
where the living tend their small fires.
Nice place to visit. Nice place,*

except for the weather, the people, the food...

Prayer at Thirty Below

Pink dawn, pink icing of snow
on the frozen lake. Even You must be cold—
the sun a pale brooch pinned to Your coat.

The trees pop their knuckles.
The baseboard heaters clatter and groan.
Smarter than we are, the ducks are long gone—

even the idiot swans left in December,
five white shirts flapping south.
Now a stiff ribbon of smoke unspools

from the powerplant. I'm lumped
on the sofa—sore throat, the tv's holler
and flash. I want to go where the swans go.

I want a blood warm sea—terra cotta mossed
on the rooftops, backwards tumble of stars.
The curtains' deep breath. The neighbor's

crackly record again—*Guantanamera*,
sad little rosary stuck in my head. I want
what everyone wants—sun on my neck

all afternoon like a fever, then sleep—
warm snow we lie down in.

Race Point Vanitas

November, seal-colored sky, the wind
a small corpse I've dragged from the parking lot,
halfway to Herring Cove. The tide's going out,

inhaling itself—wet sand ridged here and there
like a cat's mouth. The brave little boats
come and go. The waves stumble in and collapse,

two fingers of sepia haze over the mainland,
each blade of dune grass etching its circle of time
in the sand. A pale arm of sunlight pierces the clouds—

God reaching down, winding His clocks.
A gull hangs in the wind, strung from the sky's
rearview mirror. The clouds roll away

on their silent wheels. The tide's going out,
and the brave little boats. We're like them.
Smaller and smaller, then nothing but blue horizon.

Tall Ships

they call them, thick-wristed dowagers
sailing down Commercial Street,
muumuus luffing in the bay breeze.

They come from all over, adam's apples
jutting, whiskers caked in thick foundation.
They stride in tweed skirts

and bagged hose, Peter Pan collars,
scarves knotted at wattled necks—
nothing like the tittering, slim-hipped

drag queens—no spike heels, no spandex.
The wives come too, sometimes the children—
everyone tight-lipped, careful

with pronouns. *This is who we are,*
the Tall Ships announce, slowly
fixing lipstick in tiny mirrors,

this is who we've always been.
They miss their mothers, Nancy says.
Maybe it's the lingerie, I say, but that's not right.

There's what we desire, and then
there's the truth—ankle turned in its scuffed
pump, wig like a worried spaniel, slightly askew.

And what if we become the thing we love?
What still, strange pool do we drown in,
dress-backs caught in our pantyhose?

On Monday, they'll step into boxer shorts,
brown wool suits. They'll kiss their wives
goodbye, drive their bodies off

to work—fluorescent hum, the phone's
insistent chirp. Just like the rest of us,
hunkered behind our desks

while the selves we carry inside
preen all day on café chairs, sipping Campari,
gazing out at the green and sequined bay.

In the Old City

The streets are fierce with vendors' carts—
ices the color of anti-freeze, grey meat
on a stick. Everything's for sale: a green monkey

baring its fangs, stall after stall of knock-off
t-shirts, Mickey demented and leering.
You buy a pink toy broom, sweep a tiny spot

of sidewalk, the back of my hand (proletarian
toy, toy of low expectations). Quito sprawls
around us, jade bowl of smog. In each new church

the crucifixes grow more cruel, each Christ
more fervently pierced, gore-streaked, ecstatic—
gruesome work, devotion—we stop for coffee,

strong and sweet, black tincture thinned
with boiling water. A rooster strips its gears.
All the churchbells ring at once, their long call

to the saints ascending, a kind of joy, blurred
into the traffic's bellow and honk. White-wigged,
dreaming of fire, Mt. Pichincha throbs at the end

of every street. It's time to sell what we can sell,
crawl on torn knees to the steps of *La Merced*.
Time to forget this world, this sun, gold-

leafed behind our heads, almost a benediction…

Dark City

You thought you were bound for the races—
hipflask of rye, straw boater jauntily cocked.

This ain't Saratoga—this burnt horizon,
red night that licks the skyline's broken teeth.

The station reeks of meat-rot, your bootsoles
sizzle like steaks. Train after train heaves up

to the platform, disgorges, churns away empty,
the same pale conductor leering from each caboose.

You drag your valise a few blocks, check in
to Vanita's Hotel—one room down

a woman screams and screams
as if she's wild with sex, as if someone's

cutting her throat. You don't sleep,
but still these terrible dreams: your house

full of strangers—you weep, stamp your feet,
tear off your clothes. Only the dachshund

pays any mind (*Fritzie!* the man says—
Fritzie, shut up!). Well, friend—

time to unpack that valise, stroll to the bar.
The band keeps playing the Limehouse Blues.

Pretty girls dance, red mouths busy with worms.

Desiccated Mouse Found on Screen Porch

What got you, little crunch—cheez-curl
of bone and fur? Not me, though when the yellow-
jackets stung me seven times I sprayed their nest

inside the front-porch pillar—left their bright
spilled bodies on the steps, scatter of demonic beads.
And not the feral cats next door, silent

in their baggy pants—they'd eat you whole,
slurp the pink spaghetto of your tail, devour even
your tiny, meticulous teeth. Atlanta, August sump

(white sky, dogwood wilt)—yet here you are,
crisply mummified, whole down to whiskers,
toenails on curled lizard feet. Old age? Suicide?

Poison, maybe—the roach guy, the neighbor's
impossible lawn? One thing or another, I know—
mootest mootness of all. I'll sweep up your husk

in the dustpan, toss it into the backyard sumac-choke,
the crepe myrtle's pink ruin. Like some kind of sad
cosmic housemaid. Some small, incompetent god.

Insomnia Dentata

Last week I bought a dozen lily buds,
pale, clenched beaks. Three days
of slow striptease, and now they're waving

dusty penises, spritzing the room
with *eau du grandma*. What suckers we are
for transformation—Hale-Bopp

smudged above the Yankee Mart,
then dawn—the salt-bog's ghost-rind
of ice struck suddenly fuschia.

Mote drift in the lamplight, refrigerator hum—
even the stillness won't keep still.
Four a.m., the garden upholstered

in moon-blued snow, the wind
rubbing its shaggy neck against the house.
Who can sleep? Close your eyes

and the landlord's taxidermied owl
gapes from the wardrobe, ear-tufts
molting, wings wired in mid-swoop.

Close your eyes and the universe hurtles
away from itself, our lives wobble off
on their bent wheels, relentless, without us.

Ovid in Florida

All day the sky burned clear and blue
as propane—too hot to think, too hot
even in the a.c.'s chilly wheeze.

Now the wind's picking up. Across the street,
the sick banana tree flaps its green ears.
Nobody writes anymore. Nobody calls—

the City rattles off with its rusty shopping cart;
forgets you the moment you leave.
Tornado light. Dark skyline of clouds

in the west—the first fat drops of rain
ring like spent shells on the carport.
The neighbor's parrot cackles and shrieks

from their porch—some days it says *hello,*
hello, and I hope it's talking to me.
Lightning jabs the ballfield with its bent fork.

The rain falls as if it will never stop, and then
it stops. Out on the walk, an orange hornet
stings a spider the size of a child's hand,

which quivers and wilts. Sit still around here
and something will get you—
even the houseplants look hungry,

even this flamingo-colored sunset
erupting over the chemical plant,
the poached lawn, its pale ascensions of steam…

Fire Ants

Sunday, a small town
north of the driveway, modest
earthworks down in the grass.

A week later, suburban sprawl—
anthill the size of an omelet,
a baby, a toilet seat.

We pictured it cracking the walk,
heaving the big catalpa—
when they sting, someone told us,

they all sting at once, pheromones
whispering *kill, kill.*
You scalded the ants

with boiling water. Enraged,
they raced back and forth.
I sprinkled the mound

with dry grits (someone said
the workers lug them down
to the queen, who eats

and explodes)—the ants grew
fearless and strong. In the end
you drove to Wal-Mart,

bought a plunger, ankle socks,
Cheez Kurls, a black bottle of poison.
We poured the sweet-

smelling crystals. The neighbor's
tomcat yawned in the shade.
Three days later the nest was dead,

ghost town—a thousand brittle
corpses stacked nearby,
their last inscrutable work.

Well, we said. It had to be done.
And for a while we thought
of other things. Then you tracked

bright cursive through the marigolds,
found a big new burrow
near the back fence.

And last night I dreamed of ants,
ants lifting us up in our sleep,
bearing us down like gifts

to the earth's dark core.

Nursing Home

In the men's ward
senile farmers
lie in bed like sour loaves.
Rain or sun, no matter what,
it's bad for the corn.

Semi-private, Grandma scowls
or grins but can't speak, can't
move her right side. *A month,*
the doctor shrugs. *A year.*

Rain. More rain.
Mosquitos breed in the tall grass.
Out in the county
the creeks begin to rise.
Pontifical, Grandma waves
two fingers—blessing
the table, the wall—

what would she say
if God, relentless, relented?
Try to die young?
Somebody hold me?
Somebody bring me a soda?

2
Life is short, then you get old.
You moan in your sleep,
curled like a dog in a narrow bed:

pale blue diaper, bony leg
twitching. Who knows
what you're dreaming?

Wedding day.   Bingo.
New lambs on the farm.
Grandson pressing the pillow
tight to your mouth's dark slot…

Later, he waves goodbye
to the nurse. Walks out to the car
in the slow rain. Drives himself home.

1882: The Afterlife

From Texas Ranchman,
the memoirs of John A. Loomis

There was a good-sized community of blacks around San Angelo in those days—soldiers billeted up at Fort Concho, cowboys drawn to the open range, the big ranches. Among these was a man named Ellis—given or Christian name, no one knew—who fell ill and after several days expired. A large crowd gathered for the burial, the graveyard lying just across the creek from town. The sermon was long, the day frigid and bright. The preacher had finally worked his way up to the kingdom and the glory when Ellis sat bolt upright in the open casket. Damn, he said. It's cold as hell out here. The funeral-goers shrieked and bolted, men, women and children all stampeding through the icy shallows of Kickapoo Creek.

Ellis lived a long time after his death—another fifteen years. The people of Concho County called him Dead Ellis, and most would cross the street to avoid him, or make the sign of the evil eye when he passed. He lived those last fifteen years like a ghost—working all day at his forge, at sunset trudging slowly back to his shack on the edge of town—even the whores at Miss Ida's shunned him. I have no idea why he stayed in San Angelo, didn't pack up the forge and drive his old mule and buckboard off to Montana or Mexico, anywhere but Concho County. He seemed trapped there somehow, as if it were a kind of purgatory, as if the mass of his previous life had been so great that now, dead except for the fact of that breathing, walking body, his spirit could not escape its gravitational pull.

Thirty years later, my own health failing, I wonder what Ellis did to deserve that terrible sentence; that afterlife. He had been a drinking man, I know, and fearsome in a brawl owing to the great strength of his arms—but most of us drank and whored and brawled in those days, and most of us went on in the conventional way to our deserved reward, grim or otherwise. These days, I believe in the Old Testament God, white-bearded, capricious and cruel. I can think of no other way to account for Dead Ellis, the lonesome ring of his hammer all day, every night his long walk home.

In Circe's Garden

The goats have milked themselves.
The wine mulls in its jug.
A flock of terns simmers and darts
above the surf, hunting for bugs.

Mist rise. Sundown
slitting its wrists in the warm bay.
Circe lifts the oiled hair at her nape.
Prismatic, the robe sighs

from her back. None of it's real—
her ripe lips, breasts mapped
with green veins: hocus pocus—
sawdust and wax.

Beautiful sawdust. Beautiful wax.
The men snuffle and root in their sty.
Polités glares through the window,
ears twitching, a bluefly

buzzing his snout. What can I tell him—
the world is full of impossible things?
It gets better, then it gets worse?
A short sail, dark wind—

the cold mansion, Acheron weeping
into its cave. Groaning, confused,
our fathers will dust their suits
of worms, shuffle out to embrace us...

Letter from the Cardiac Unit

Cigarettes. Drinking. One last hit of acid
back in 1989. Who knows why my heart
jitters off on its own like this—

not the tanned cardiologist, not the pretty intern
who, late last night, pushed a KY'd finger
up my ass for reasons of her own

(my *heart*, I tried to tell her, half asleep
and stoned on Xanax—it's my *heart*).
I'm wired, pierced—the monitor's green line

snaggles and bleeps, the i.v. drips heparin
into the back of my hand. The old man
in the next bed doesn't look so good,

pinched in the tv's mushroom light.
There's nothing on in the next life, either—
all Charlton Heston, all the time.

2
Inheritance. Karma. What I deserve.
Old Invisible walks the halls,
shakes up his jar of souls, peers in.

3
My heart is a fluttering, naked thing.
It wants to leap from its lattice of ribs,
fly down the corridor, never come back.

Last night something flashed
in my head, then my room was quick
with doctors, frowning over their stethoscopes.

Gossamer, lace—the skin that keeps
this world from leaking into the next.
One minute you're forking a cube

of green Jell-O; next you're motoring off
in your ghost car, turn signal blinking.

4
I want to come back as a harbor seal.
I want to catch a glittering fish in my teeth,
sleep all afternoon on the sand. October,

twilight, sunset burnt to its last magenta strip—
I'll be the dark, inquisitive head in the swell.
Old friend, I'll say. *Unzip that earnest skin.*

The water's cold. Come swim with me.

THREE

The Past

When Uncle Chet died, they found a note
in his desk—*give Jon the videos.* A big box
arrived by UPS, fifty-seven tapes, all hard-core—

Truck Stop Sluts, Dirty Debutantes, China Silk.
I was thirty-five, just divorced. He knew
I'd watch them, the kid who'd rifled his *Playboys*,

knew I'd sit for two days straight, drinking scotch,
fast-forwarding the dialogue—a kind of wake.
Sex is the biggest nothing of all time, Warhol said,

but Chet didn't think so, alone the last few years
in his La-Z-Boy, pacemaker ticking.
The women were mostly blonde, pubic hair

pruned into spun-gold strips, breasts firm
as mangoes, nipples always erect. *The biggest
nothing of all time*, I thought, half-drunk,

half-dozed on the couch: friction, hydraulics—
someone's pimply buttocks always churning.
Labial twilight out in the garden, tape whir

in the gobbling slot. The camera wobbled,
panned out (elbow, flare of hip, small
square chin), the blurred and glistening parts

merged into a girl I swear I recognized,
she'd haunted high school's dim periphery,
dimpled and busty, pregnant at seventeen—

I called her a name once, clever boy,
and she cried. Nose job. Breast job.
Hair lacquered and swooped—still, I'm almost sure

it was her, kneeling, taking one man after another
into her mouth. Forget what you've planned,
what you know. Your life's veering off on its own—

brakes failed, back seat on fire. There's a dark
house ahead, everyone you've ever known inside.
Close your eyes. Drive as fast as you can.

Uncle

Late summer, football in the Hadleys' yard,
dogpack of neighborhood boys. We squabbled
even more than usual—like hell the plaster deer

was out of bounds, bull*shit* the score was tied,
until Rex Hadley called my older brother
a pussy. *You're* the pussy, I said, spindly
nine-year-old, rusty faucet squeak. In five years

Rex would ship out to Okinawa, lose both legs
in a jeep-wreck. Mink-eyed, thick, blond fuzz
on his lip—he socked my gut and blacked my eye,

pinned me facedown in the bug-worked grass
before I threw a single punch. *Say uncle*
he hissed, slamming my face harder and harder
into the dirt—mouthful of blood, cicada whine

in my left ear. Fireflies short-circuited
the apple trees. My brother stood a few feet away.
And told me to say it. *Say uncle. Don't be a fool.*

Pneumonia, 1969

Mostly I slept.
Or watched the cat
watch nothing

hover just above my bed.
My brother glued
his model planes.

Spitfires, Hellcats—
they roared out the window,
came stuttering back

riddled, in flames.
The sky turned green.
The rain fell

all at once. My mother
sang in the kitchen,
fingered the knives.

I looked through the window
and saw myself—pale,
sheet pulled up to my chin.

The poplars steamed.
I flew above Roosevelt Drive
in my underpants,

flapping my arms.
The town like a train-set
below me: little cars,

little houses. My father
sipping his drink
on the sagged deck.

His empty shirts
convulsing on the line.

Camping Trip

That year we slept on Winston smoke
and bourbon from my father's lungs—
the rubber mattresses alive

and blind inside the tent like larvae.
The Coleman lantern breathed
until my father coughed it out.

The crickets whetted their tiny knives.
Look out look out look out!
my father yelled in his sleep—

his old dream of the war: camped
in an open field, tanks crawling
the ridge. My mother crooned,

tried to comfort him. I want to say
they made love, straining, quiet
in the musty tent, their zipped-

together sleeping bags—
but how would I know? I slept.
Deer Creek was a cocktail party,

its dozen voices boozy and glad
in the dark. And then the bear
snuffled out of the woods.

It shredded the styrofoam cooler,
lapped up the milk, devoured
the bacon and eggs. *Keep still*

my father hissed, the bear
grunting and belching outside—
don't make a sound! Fool boy,

raised on Batman, Bonanza—
what did I think? He'd burst
from the tent in the pre-dawn fade,

kill the bear with his pocket knife?
The crickets honed. My father
coughed, then wheezed.

Every night of his life, something
was out there. Nosing the tent-flaps,
leaving its clawed tracks in the dirt.

This Poet's Life: A Memoir

We lived on a hill in a small town.
    We seemed a normal family—
        mother and father, two young sons.

Well. That summer was long and hot.
    Father spoke to us sharply
        more than once. The Hadleys' youngest

daughter liked to sunbathe nude—
    I spied on her with Mom's binoculars.
        I learned to drive—a crucial day

in all our lives. I wrecked the family
    wagon, twice. *What in the world
        were you thinking?* my father said—

nearly spilling his drink. Scarring me for life.

Interiors

I live in a small house.
The door's locked—
I can't leave

and no one comes in.
I look through the keyhole:
sometimes a brick wall,

the ocean, a sky
quick with birds.
Sometimes an eye

looking back. I grow old.
I look through the keyhole
again, and there's death.

She jangles her keys.
Sets her meathook down,
opens the door.

We walk out,
crossing a field of weeds.
We lie down

in the Johnson grass,
in the chicory
and Queen Anne's lace.

I tell her I've waited—
how faithful I've been.

Regret

Mosquitos invade
on their jet-skis. The moon
hangs itself in the orchard,

eyes bugged, mouth a dark "O."
Move fast enough, Einstein said,
and time stops—the last thing

anyone wants. I'm keeping still:
nap on the futon, supper
of olives and cheese.

Let the clock squat on the mantle,
adding one and one to what's past…

Damage

I've been thinking a lot about love;
bomb in the market,
random and cruel.

I'd like to explain a few things,
but the loose flap in my brain
keeps nothing out, nothing in.

It's late, the night's little springs
winding down. Asleep,
weightless, translucent—

you sign a dark truce
with the past. Beautiful corpse
lugged on your back.

Glittering stone in your shoe.

Peace

Armpit draggle of spanish moss in the trees,
dawn's fuchsia burn, slight hum.

Six a.m., someone revs a leaf-blower—
6:15 and the whole subdivision's whooshing

the few sad leaves from lawn to lawn.
This is *so* not home, as my students would say

if they weren't all from here,
if they'd say anything, which mostly

they won't. Back in Provincetown
the ocean's winter pale, the pilings along the bay

glow green in the fadelight; seaglass, verdigris—
whole other palette, whole other life.

The leaf blowers whine. Next door, ecstatic,
the parrot shrieks from its porch. Every dog

in Cherry Creek begins to howl at once; then
you hear the firetruck dopplering west on 39th:

she-wolf, moving fast: *eat the people, run with me.*

Mis en Abime

There now, said the Irish nurse
soothing a strand of hair
from your eyes, checking

the rubber straps that pinned
your wrists. Outside, mist-smear,
sheep-blur on the green hill.

The thing that made you wild
slept in its den, only its fox-eyed
shadow crossing your face

at twilight, slow as thorazine.
In the old half-dream, half-memory
you're nine, standing in a square

of sunlight, mote drift up
from green shag, livingroom doused
in Glade. *Kate*, your father says,

*think about this: could the sun
be a dream? The window? The girl?*
You want to run outside, jump

onto your bike, pedal away—
but the world's too gorgeous
and flat. Backdrop

you're painted into: mountains,
thin sky, girl lost in the woods…

In the Mirror It Is Sunday

and the new poem's reducing itself to sex and death,
as they all do, if that's a reduction, which maybe it isn't.

Back arched, one slim wrist behind her neck, she bites
the fat black plum—bright wedge of late morning sun

through the curtain-gap, golden fuzz on her thigh.
Nice little breakdown I'm having, late morning,

late summer, James Brown on the boombox—
good *God*—the day unwinding around us,

movie spilled from its reel. Year of the vain promise,
car wreck, day lilies bent from last night's rain.

2
No more dog metaphors, I keep telling myself.
Oh arrhythmia, three-legged dog—ten years

you've dactylled along at my side, followed me
out to the mailbox, parked your sorry ass at my feet.

Now I'm weepy from too much Xanax
(the juice is red, the juice runs down her arm),

the green silk panties phosphorescing on the floor.
I don't know what it means to wake up anymore,

as if I'd taken the wrong train—the landscape
rushing past the window terribly foreign,

terribly new. She bites the plum. The juice runs
down her arm. In the mirror nothing's changed,

the driveway steams, a mockingbird riffs—
half-bar of woodthrush, lick of spotted wren.

3
In the mirror it is Sunday, the breakfast plates
conspire in the sink, the day-moon's thin rationale

chalked above the pine-tops. In the mirror it is Sunday
but the poem won't pay attention—it's in love

with the plum, the red juice, her small sharp teeth…

Misfit Farm

I am the burro-pig, the cow with a small twin
half-grown from its hip, the llama-thing
with wrong eyes. The only one of my kind,

thank God—God's inscrutable joke. You are the girl
with lobster hands, the dog whose two heads snarl
and snap at themselves. We must never mate.

We'll graze a while, flank to neck.
Observe the dust-plume hauled by the rattling truck.
Feel the bright green hum of this electric fence.

November

I should rake the sepia crunch
of dogwood leaves, set them out
in tall, forlorn bags at the curb.

I should water the whimpering
houseplants—not their fault
their little lives oppress me,

not their fault I want them dead.
Some days I don't speak,
not even to the neighbor's cat

lolled again on the back porch,
cold rag of sun. Solitude,
green-skinned and glistening—

I wrap you around my neck
each morning, proud, a little afraid.

Sex

It's good, Uncle Id would say, to live
in these bodies, walk them around
the frozen lake, sit them down by the birch-

log fire, fat book and whiskey-glass,
dinner soon and sleep soon, deer and red fox
writing the past outside in the snow—

here's where we were, and here and here.
The Tao says live in the moment, stop
wanting—easy for old Lao Tzu,

who never cupped your breasts
inside a cashmere blouse, never
licked your knee-pit's lavender spice.

Wind-surf in the pines, squirrel flounce
across the snow-enameled lawn;
if you were here, you'd perch a hand

on the chairback, step one foot and then
the other out of your shrugged nightgown.
Alone, I doze on the couch. The room

fills with snow. I shovel all night,
but the room keeps filling with snow.

Ars Poetica

It's not the dog, or even the ghost
of the dog, but the ghost of the dog's
lean shadow, camera obscura sketched

on the canvas—the north window's
steeped light not the light in the painting,
the girl in the painting not the girl

on the chair, the ghost of the light
and the girl deep in Vermeer's dust,
the ghost of the shadow of the ghost

of the girl in our heads, walking home
through the twilight's blue fade,
the painting alive on its dark wall,

the poem alive but asleep on the page,
till you, dear reader (how are you?),
open the book and fall in,

ghost, shadow and dog. The book's almost
over, here's my advice: put it down,
go to bed, wake up your wife.

Tell her you can't sleep. Tell her all day
you writhe on the cross of desire.

Deer Hit

You're seventeen and tunnel-vision drunk,
swerving your father's Fairlane wagon home

at 3:00 a.m. Two-lane road, all curves
and dips—dark woods, a stream, a patchy acre

of teazle and grass. You don't see the deer
till they turn their heads—road full of eyeballs,

small moons glowing. You crank the wheel,
stamp both feet on the brake, skid and jolt

into the ditch. Glitter and crunch of broken glass
in your lap, deer hair drifting like dust. Your chin

and shirt are soaked—one eye half-obscured
by the cocked bridge of your nose. The car

still running, its lights angled up at the trees.
You get out. The deer lies on its side.

A doe, spinning itself around
in a frantic circle, front legs scrambling,

back legs paralyzed, dead. Making a sound—
again and again this terrible bleat.

You watch for a while. It tires, lies still.
And here's what you do: pick the deer up

like a bride. Wrestle it into the back of the car—
the seat folded down. Somehow, you steer

the wagon out of the ditch and head home,
night rushing in through the broken window,

headlight dangling, side-mirror gone.
Your nose throbs, something stabs

in your side. The deer breathing behind you,
shallow and fast. A stoplight, you're almost home

and the deer scrambles to life, its long head
appears like a ghost in the rearview mirror

and bites you, its teeth clamp down on your shoulder
and maybe you scream, you struggle and flail

till the deer, exhausted, lets go and lies down.

2
Your father's waiting up, watching tv.
He's had a few drinks and he's angry.

Christ, he says, when you let yourself in.
It's Night of the Living Dead. You tell him

some of what happened: the dark road,
the deer you couldn't avoid. Outside, he circles

the car. *Jesus*, he says. A long silence.
Son of a bitch, looking in. He opens the tailgate,

drags the quivering deer out by a leg.
What can you tell him—you weren't thinking,

you'd injured your head? You wanted to fix
what you'd broken—restore the beautiful body,

color of wet straw, color of oak leaves in winter?
The deer shudders and bleats in the driveway.

Your father walks to the toolshed,
comes back lugging a concrete block.

Some things stay with you. Dumping the body
deep in the woods, like a gangster. The dent

in your nose. All your life, the trail of ruin you leave.

NOTES

ONE

"Romance: A Parable": For Brandy Kershner.

"You Blow Out the Candles": For Charles Wright.

"Epithalamial": For AMC.

"Russian Novel": For Sidney Wade.

"Uncle Chester's Second Wife": Chet and Cathy are entirely fictitious. As is the narrative.

TWO

"Tourists": The line from Thoreau is paraphrased.

"Tall Ships": Refers to Provincetown's annual October cross-dressing festival.

"Ovid in Florida": For Ann LeZotte.

"Dead Ellis": Adapted from a memoir written by my great-great-uncle, who owned and operated a cattle ranch in Concho County, Texas through the 1880s. He was an avid shooter and sportsman, and built the first nine-hole golf course west of the Pecos there in 1891. The ranch went bankrupt in 1893.

THREE

"Sex": Uncle Id is Whitman.

"Damage": For Caitlin McDonnell.

"In the Mirror It Is Sunday": The title is a line from Paul Celan's "Love Crown."

"Ars Poetica": Refers to a line from Charles Wright's essay "Improvisations on Form and Measure."

"Deer Hit": For David Young.

ACKNOWLEDGMENTS

I wish to express my gratitude to the editors of these fine journals, in which the listed poems have appeared:

Conduit: "Interiors."

Crazyhorse: "In the Old City," "The Past," "Prayer at Thirty Below," "Tall Ships," "Uncle Chester's Second Wife."

Dickinson Review: "Damage," "Peace," "Uncle."

FIELD: "Addictions," "Ars Poetica," "Deer Hit," "Happiness," "Insomnia Dentata," "In the Mirror It Is Sunday," "Letter from the Cardiac Unit," "On the First Tee with Charles Wright," "Ovid in Florida," "Romance: A Parable," "Sex," "Tourists."

Gettysburg Review: "Skinnydipping, Late Summer" (as "Skinny-dipping at Forty"), "You Blow Out the Candles."

Iowa Review: "Balthus Returns."

The New Republic: "In Circe's Garden."

Tikkun: "Sin."

Virginia Quarterly Review: "Longing," "The Pleasure Principle."

Particular thanks to the editors of FIELD, and to the Corporation of Yaddo for providing the time and space in which many of these poems were written. I am grateful also to John Allman, Iris Guillemette, Jesse Lee Kercheval, Brandy Kershner, Dr. Jonathan Langberg and his trusty Zapmaster 2000, Fred Leebron, William Logan, Gloria Loomis, Gail Mazur, Caitlin McDonnell, Lorrie Moore, Greg Orr, Col. Padgett Powell, Nancy Reisman, Donald and June Roberts, Jane Shore, Dr. Sidney Wade, David Walker, Ron Wallace, Charles Wright, and David Young—you've all been very kind.